Proceeds from this book will be donated to Billy's sons and to help others suffering from domestic violence.

Wise Choice

HIS FIANCE KILLED HIM JUST HOURS BEFORE
THE WEDDING, WHAT HAPPEN, WHY? WAS THERE
ANOTHER MAN? HOW COULD LOVE TURN TO HATE?
MOM KILLS DAD WITH CHILDREN WATCHING.

Mrs Barbara Jean Obas

Copyright © 2014 Mrs Barbara Jean Obas
All rights reserved.
ISBN-13: 9780615959696
ISBN-10: 0615959695

I am dedicating this book to Billy R. Brewster and his sons, William Raphael Brewster, Billy Raphael Brewster Jr., and Anthony Irvin, whom he loved and had high hopes for. These young lives are forever changed.

To Billy: thank you for thirty-six years of love, strength, and determination. You always gave this family more than you could have imagined. We know God has promised we will see each other again in eternity. Thank you, my son, for all your gifts you have left us: your beautiful children, your wonderful smile, your sense of humor, and, most of all, your *love*.

See you soon, my child, in God's eternity.

Until then, Mother

Contents

Prelude ix
    The Beginning 1
    Off to Chicago 4
    The Move 6
    The First Day at a New School 7
    Billy Being Billy 10
    School Backfire 12
    The Runaway 17
    The Mistake 18
    The Indictment 21
    The Separation 24
    Truck Driving 27
    NaCola Enters Our Lives 28
Karen's Passing 31
    A New Life 35
    The Vacation 41
    Mama, Please Don't Be Late! 44
    The Wedding 46
    The News 49
    The Confession 50
    Saying Good-Bye 54
    The Family's Prepared Wisdom Statements 58
    Conclusion 61

Prelude

I write this book to remember my third-born son, Billy Raphael Brewster. He lived, loved, and was loved. Billy was a son, grandson, father, brother, nephew, and uncle. Working long hours to support his family, he earned what money he had by being a truck driver. His life, dreams, and hopes were not taken by a driving accident or robbery; they were stolen from him by his bride-to-be on his wedding night. This was domestic violence; this was an unnecessary murder.

Some may ask, "Why are you writing a book?" I answer that I believe our purpose on this earth is to help someone from our own life experiences. I have realized the significant impact one person can have on the lives of those around them. If Billy's story inspires even one person to resolve their disagreements in a peaceful manner, then I thank God that Billy's life made a difference. My story starts with so much love from a family who had hopes and dreams—and ends in domestic violence.

Often, domestic violence is directed toward women. But the reality is that entire families are affected by domestic violence—husbands, wives, even children. No one wants to shed light on such an ugly problem, so all too often, it is not talked about. America, now is the time to stand up and end the violence. Proceeds from this book will go toward those affected by domestic violence, including a trust fund for Billy's children.

The Beginning

August 17, 1975

We lived in Hollis, Queens, on the first floor of a two-family apartment with my husband at the time, Walter Brewster, and my five- and six-year-old sons, David Walter Jr., and Walter Jr.—and one on the way. I remember the night that Billy made his entrance into the world. It was 2:00 a.m. I went to the bathroom and was shocked to find that the baby was close to being born, yet I had not felt any pain or contractions. Carefully, I made my way back to the couch and told my husband to call 911. He was upset, saying, "You are a grown woman—why did you not go to the hospital before now?"

"Call nine-one-one; this child is coming, and he is coming now!" I screamed back.

When the police arrived, I was 9.5 centimeters dilated. Whether we were ready for it or not, this baby was coming.

The officer said, "Get the ambulance—the baby is coming now." He turned to me and gave me instructions. "Push. Don't stand up. Just push." One push and a big gush of water later, our third son, Billy, arrived. Walter and I were hoping for a girl this time, but I was more than happy with another son. However, shortly after Billy's birth, Walter and I separated. From the very beginning, Billy was a busy baby, filled with curiosity. He began to talk at two years old, and when he was three, I married Richard Mccann. It was evident that Billy was all boy, often giving his older brothers a run for their money. As he grew up, he became a daredevil, riding his Big Wheels onto the street, eating his brothers' snacks, and wearing their clothes. He would be my baby for ten years.

In the third grade, Richard and I decided that Billy should go to the Catholic school St. John's, because schools in our area of Far Rockaway, New York, were becoming crowded. One day, I came home from work to find Billy waiting for me. He told me that a nun told him the only way to get to heaven was through our Lord, Jesus Christ. I said, "Yes, Billy, I understand that to be the truth."

"But Mama," he replied, "what about the rest of the world, who believe in something else? What about Muslims, Buddhists, Jews, and the Five Percenters? Do they all go to hell?"

I replied, "Yes, I believe that is what the Bible says." Billy asked once again, "Mama, does that make sense to you? Three-fourths of the world will go to hell. Are you trying to tell me heaven is for white people and to hell with the rest?"

I thought a moment before I said, "Now, son, I never thought of it that way, but I believe the Bible."

Shortly after this exchange, Billy decided to be a Muslim. He even changed his name to Wise B. God. One day after school, he informed me that he would no longer eat pork. I said, "Billy, I can see some hungry days ahead of you."

He was adamant. "Mother, my name is Wise; respect me enough to call me by my name."

Billy loved to talk, be in the spotlight, and read everything he could get his hands on, especially relating to the Muslim culture. Joining the Muslim culture gave Billy a platform to engage in serious conversations. I remember thinking that as long as he was reading, I could endure the turbulence of the ride. I was confident that he would find his way as long as he continued to read.

Billy was the baby of the family for ten years. He loved being the baby. When there were chores to be completed around the house, he would remind me he was the baby and should not have to do any chores. He would tease his older brothers, telling them they missed a spot while washing dishes or pointing out where the rug needed to be vacuumed. Billy was a true baby brother!

One night before his tenth birthday, I told him we were going to have another child. He became very upset and stopped answering to his name. After his sister, Dawn Essence, was born, he seemed distanced and unhappy. One day, I took him out for ice cream. I explained to him that he was still my baby boy and that his sister, Dawn, was the baby girl. It was evident that Billy did not want to share the spotlight, but after some time, he adjusted to his little sister's place in the family.

Billy always tried to make himself more visible. He would correct me if I addressed him as Billy. "Why is it so important that I call you Wise?" I asked one day.

"Mommy, just because you don't know about the Muslims and others doesn't mean they are going to hell. Ali changed his name, and his family respected his choices. Now the man is rich. I bet no one calls him Cassius Clay now!" he exclaimed.

"Good point," I said. "I will call you Wise when you become a rich man." We both laughed.

Over the next few years, Billy kept up with his newfound religion. He would be Wise to God, friends, and family.

Billy was growing into his role as big brother. He would play with his little sister and watch her in the yard. He would teach her to pick up his things, bring him water and soda, and wait on him. Being a big brother had some advantage s. Then, I had to tell him we were having another baby. I still remember calling him into the kitchen. He had a puzzled look on his face.

"What's up, Mama?"

I tried to seem upbeat. "Wise, you are about to be a big brother again!" I remember how betrayed he looked.

"Another baby? I cannot believe you are telling me this. Boy or girl?"

"I am not sure."

"I guess I am not your baby."

"Billy, don't be upset."

His little brother, Warren, soon arrived. By this time, Billy was already fourteen years old. Walter Jr. was in the navy, and his wife, Yvette, was expecting their first child. When their baby, Warren III, was still very young, Billy came home and said, "Mama, I just realized that you are having children the same time as your children. Lil' Warren will be an uncle before he is one year old. Is that even legal?"

I told him, "It is, I hope. Billy, it will work out; trust me."

Off to Chicago

I worked the night shift, and when I would go to work, Billy thought that it was his time to roam New York streets. Knowing how unsafe that was, I called my oldest brother, Curtis. I explained the problems I was having with my third son. Brother Curtis jokingly said, "You must send the lad to me." He was an army sergeant and Vietnam veteran. "I will either straighten him our or lay him out—that will be his choice." I put him on the next plane to Chicago.

Eventually, Billy grew to respect and love his uncle, but this took some time. For a few months, Billy teamed up with his cousin Nick. They would test and try to fool Uncle Curtis, but being a country boy, he was able to stay one step ahead of them.

One night, Billy called me and said in a low voice, "Mommy, I think Uncle Curtis is practicing witchcraft."

"Why do you say that, son?"

"There is no way he could know what a brother is thinking. What the hell—the man is up at four o'clock every morning and doesn't come home till after four in the afternoon. He comes home with all these country sayings. I'll be thinking about hooking up with Cousin Nick, when he looks at me and out of the blue says, 'Billy, you ain't going nowhere.' How does he know this without witchcraft? The man has a wife and seven kids, and out of the blue, he picks up on what I'm thinking? Mommy, this is not natural." He was laughing by now.

"Billy, you should stop thinking so loud," I said.

"I guess you are right."

♦ ♦ ♦

Billy returned home after a year or so. He had grown up somewhat. After a few days, he got right back to being a Five Percenter. He had gone undercover in Chicago. He knew his Uncle Curtis would be opposed to his Muslim ways. He resumed not eating pork.

"Billy, did you eat pork in Chicago?" I asked.

"Mama, if I had stopped eating pork in Chi-town, I would have starved to death," Billy explained. "In Chicago, they barbecue everything. They even use the same pot and grill for everything. So yes, when I was in Chicago, I was forced to eat swine. They have swine in milk. This is crazy. No wonder why black people have high blood pressure, diabetes, and heart disease. Mama, it's their diet. Look in the hood—a liquor store at every corner, a barbecue joint, and a church. Mama, that is real life.

"Mama, I am older now. You will be my mama. Please call me by my name."

"What name is that, my son?"

"Wise, by God," he answered.

"First, tell me what it means."

"Well, as a black man, I was made in God's image, and as so, I too am a god," he explained. "Mama, this is what I believe. Can you respect that?"

"OK son, let me tell you what I believe. Jesus Christ died for our sins; he rose from his grave for our sins; and he sits on the right hand of this father."

"Mama, is it OK for us to disagree?"

"I guess," I responded.

He soon left to go out with his friends.

The Move

When my husband, Richard, and I began having marital problems, I decided to leave New York and move to Pennsylvania. The plan was set. I would take Richard out of town with the pretense of working on the relationship. I had hired a moving truck to come to my house while we were gone. My son David, my daughter-in-law Yvette, and Dean would pack up the three-bedroom house. We could not risk telling the blabbermouth, Wise, By God, aka Billy.

David said that when the truck pulled up in front of the house, Billy was jumping up and down. "Why did Mommy not tell me?" David told him to pack his stuff; there was no time to talk. They were not sure if I could keep Richard away long enough to finish the move. Billy was surprised; he had lived at the Deerfield address most of his childhood. He packed up his stuff and helped load the truck. I took Richard to the Poconos and left him at the hotel. I then went to greet my family in our new home. I had found a house in the country. It was a four-bedroom split-level on two-and-a-half acres with a small barn.

Billy was the first one out of the truck, and he was smiling. "Mama, we live here? What about the KKK? Mama, what the hell are you thinking?" He started fussing with his brother David. "How long did you know about this shit? Why did no one tell me? Am I not part of this family?"

No one said a word at first. Finally, David and I looked at each other, and at the same time, we said, "Because you have a big mouth, Billy." We laughed a lot over the next few weeks.

The First Day at a New School

Dawn was starting first grade. Billy was a freshman in high school. Billy was nervous. He had gone to the school the week before to register, and the kids had received him well. However, his actual first day could be completely different with all the new people and the not knowing what to expect. He ended up getting along well with the other students and making many friends. He had a personality and a smile that could charm anyone—and charm he did. Although he had many friends, he was suspicious of everything and everyone.

"Mama, are you aware that we are the only black kids at school?" he asked.

"Billy, has anyone threatened you or made you feel unwelcome?" I responded.

"No, Mama, they are a little bit too nice. That doesn't mean that at any time, the KKK won't show up. Mama, you spent time in Arkansas. This isn't funny. You think this is a joke. I wonder what you would do if they had a hanging. This shit isn't funny at all."

"Billy, it's not that serious. You are there to learn, not to keep bringing all that old stuff up. The world is changing. People don't think that way anymore. This is a small town; people are trying to pay their bills, not worry about how many black children are in the school. Keep thinking that dumb stuff. Billy, you are being silly."

◆ ◆ ◆

Soon, he had friends with cars picking him up before and after school. He seemed to relax a little. Girls called all the time. He told his new friends

Mrs Barbara Jean Obas

that he was related to the rappers in New York. The kids loved rap music, so they wanted to be seen with this famous relative. Billy had found a new spotlight. He was always on the phone. Of course, this was before cell phones. The house telephone was his vehicle.

A few weeks passed. The kids were enjoying school. Billy had become very popular and had stopped all the Klan jokes. He had become close with some friends and was always giving them advice. One day, he came home very quiet. He had a puzzled look on his face. He was not smiling and seemed distant.

"Son, is everything OK?" I asked.

He looked at me and said, "Mama, please tell me the truth. Are you in the Federal Witness Protection Program?"

"Billy, what are you talking about?"

That's when I saw him smiling. "Mama, no way in hell would a black woman who picked cotton in Arkansas, escaped the gangs in Chicago, lived for a time in Canada, and lived in New York for twenty-five years move here without the government having a hand in this."

"Billy, are you finished? Stop joking. Now, all jokes aren't funny. I would hate for that rumor to get started."

"Mama, rumor? Hell, that's the only thing that makes sense."

"Boy, you better go somewhere. Stop joking."

Billy had his friends thinking he was involved with gangsters in New York and Chicago, that he knew drug dealers from those cities. He displayed himself as a big wheel from the hood, and being black was all he needed to be. If someone upset him, he would threaten to send for some of his guys to put the person in check and that someone must have informed the school and the school informed the police. They told him to bring in a large amount of marijuana to school. The problem was he was unable to deliver because he never knew any big drug dealers. But Billy, being Billy, wanted spotlight on him. He could lose face because he wanted to keep the kids interested in his stories. My stepson, Chris, tried to tell my new husband, Antoine, and me what was going on. When I questioned Billy, he said, "Mama, the only reason these clowns believe me is because I am black. Mama, they want to believe that we sell drugs. Ten million people in New York, and they think I know every black person there. That shit is crazy."

"Billy, stop lying. It's going to get your ass in trouble one day."

"Why? They are so stupid. I can be stupid, too."

"Billy, stop. Just stop acting a damn fool."

"OK, Mommy, if that's what you think."

As if he could lose the attention.

Billy Being Billy

One snowy night, I decided to call off work. Billy came to my room. "Are you all right?" he asked. I told him I wasn't feeling well. "Mama, let me make you some tea. Do you want cake with that? We already cleaned the house. Mama, I hate you working night shift." He just kept talking. He seemed somewhat nervous. *God, I am not that sick,* I thought. "Mommy, don't go downstairs. I am trying to wash clothes. Dawn and I already finished the laundry. Do you want anything to eat or drink?"

I remember thinking how attentive he was being. *Wow—a clean house, the laundry finished, and cooking.* "Billy, you are being so wonderful. This should make me suspicious."

"Mama, there you go again. I love you. You work too hard. Can't a son take care of his mother without you thinking I'm up to something? Damn, I expect this from white folks, but my own mama? Damn, Mama."

"Baby, Mama's sorry. I love you."

"I love you, too." Then, he took me to my room, put me in bed, and asked, "Mommy, do you need anything else?"

"No, son, I'll just go to sleep now, OK?"

"Love you, Mommy," he said. Then, he added, "You really hurt my feelings."

"I'm sorry, son. You know I love you."

"OK, Mommy. I love you, too. Just go to sleep."

He closed the door. I could hear him telling the other children to be quiet. I lay there about thirty minutes, but then my eyes popped open. My mind said something was up, but what? I got out of bed, looked out the window, and could see footsteps in the snow-covered driveway. Hmm... hot damn. Something *was* up. I got up and went downstairs.

Billy heard me walking. He met me at the stairs. "Mama, what are you doing up? I just put you to bed. Please tell me this is not about you not trusting me. Mama, just go back to bed."

"Billy, if I didn't know better, I would say you had a girl here."

"Is that what you think?"

I was just playing, but I decided to check the closets anyway. First, I checked the one by the stairs. Then, I checked in Billy's room. I screamed, and a half-dressed girl screamed.

Billy just started laughing. "Damn, Mommy."

"Billy, you send them schoolgirls home."

"Mommy, I just put you to bed. Damn, Mommy. Why the hell don't you just sleep?" I could see him still laughing.

"Billy, did you hear me? Send them little sluts home."

"Mommy, I am taking care of that. Now, will you let me handle this? Damn, Mommy."

School Backfire

By now, Billy had become a little celebrity at school. His fellow students were buying him lunch, picking him up for school, bringing him home, and going to the games. He made his blackness count. He wore his pants hanging low, adopted a New York accent, and tried to portray a real gangster.

"Billy, you need to stop before this foolishness backfires on you. What are you up to anyway?" I asked.

"Mommy, you wanted to go to the country school with white folks. I try to do that and live a little, too, and you still aren't happy. You're always suspicious. Can't you trust me? Trust is all I ask for—just a little trust. Those white folks trust me more than my own mama. Damn."

♦ ♦ ♦

A few weeks later, my husband and I were called to the school. Billy was to go before a board. The school board wanted to expel him from school for selling weed. I had to get a lawyer. He had not finished high school yet. I knew that he didn't know any drug people, so why were they accusing Billy?

After school, a few of Billy's friends came by the house. I could see them talking. Billy seemed nervous. I had heard that another student named Frank something had accused Billy as the pusher. That night, when I questioned Billy, he got uptight. "Mommy, I am a black man. Of course I am a drug dealer."

"Billy, I believe it's more than that. I have been a black woman for more than fifty years, and I have never been accused of being a dealer of anything."

"Funny. Funny, you love those white people. Why can't you be on my side just once?"

Later that day, his friend returned. They were in the front of my house, laughing and talking loud. I heard someone say, *"Press Enterprise."* That was our local newspaper.

I walked outside and asked, "What's going on?"

All the boys stopped talking.

I said, "Please, please tell me you didn't start any trouble at school."

One of the boys said, "Sorry, I cannot tell you that!"

"Please tell me this did not get in from the *Press Enterprise*."

Again, he said, "I can't tell you that."

"I hope you guys didn't bother Frank."

"I cannot tell you that."

"What can you tell me?"

While Billy had been home from school all day, all his friends had decided to avenge his accuser. I told them to leave.

Billy was smiling. "Now, Mama, I was here with you and Grandma all day. I bet they will find some way to blame the black man."

"Billy, you are full of shit."

"My own mama don't believe me when she was with me all day. Is it my fault what these kids do? Mommy, they are going to blame me no matter what."

"Billy, just stop."

"OK, Mommy. Believe what you want to. You were always on the other side. Damn, I was home with you and Grandma. I cannot be responsible for what others do, OK?"

After going through the meeting at school, we discovered Billy had been lying about knowing big drug dealers. He could not get his hands on drugs if his life depended on it. So, I decided that when the trial was over, we would send Billy to New York to finish high school. He would live with his Grandma and Grandpa.

◆ ◆ ◆

Billy finished high school in New York and became interested in becoming an EMT. He was working and dating. He loved being an adult. "Mommy, I love having my own room. It's small, but I can walk around naked if I want. No one telling me to wash dishes or get dressed or asking me who is in my room," he joked.

"OK," I said. "I hope you can put clothes on when I come by to visit."

"You better call first!" Billy exclaimed.

◆ ◆ ◆

Billy was still Wise B. God. He went back to his Five Percenters. During that time, he met his first true love, Ms. Karen Vassel. They met at the airport where they both worked. Karen called him Wise, and he loved when she referred to him that way. She and Billy spent most of their time together.

Billy started complaining about how many hours he worked and that his take-home pay was just not enough. "Damn, Mommy, even if I claimed six people, my take-home pay would not be shit."

My mom, Billy's grandmother, decided to relocate to Pennsylvania to be near me. She rented her house in New York to Billy and Karen. He was on top of the world. Billy and Karen planned to have a baby. When they announced that Karen was expecting, he said to me, "Mama, Karen and I are planning to have a child."

"Planning?" I remember asking.

"Yes, Mama, we planned our child." Wearing his boyish grin, he said, "Mama, did you not plan Walter and David?"

"No, son, none of you were planned. I was surprised as hell. I went to see the doctor, and he said, 'You're pregnant.' What? Damn."

"Shit, Mommy, stop playing," he said.

"Son, trust me. I never planned anyone. Do not tell anyone else that," I told him.

"See, Mom, Karen and I planned our child. Now, if I could find a way to make some more money…"

"Grandma let you rent the house. Be thankful for that. Baby, I am very happy for you and Karen and your planned baby." I knew in my heart this would be a hard pregnancy for Karen because her health was not good. Karen suffered from sickle-cell anemia.

Billy and Karen were so excited and happy; I just prayed that everything would work out. Karen did have a hard time during her pregnancy, but no matter how difficult it was for her, she showed so much joy; she was always smiling. I've never seen a happier mother-to-be. Billy, aka Wise B. God, was on top of the world. He would now be a father just like his older brothers, who each had a son of their own.

Billy continued to try to make fast money. He had taken someone out of town when Karen went into labor. Baby William was very early, weighing only 2.1 pounds at birth. Karen's mother called me. "Barbara, you have a new grandson." Her voice was happy but cautious. He was very small but had strong lungs. All I could feel was joy. I had to reach Billy. He had taken those people out of town and was unaware that Karen had delivered his baby. There were no cell phones then, so I had to wait for Billy to check in. I called my mom, and we prayed for our newest little family member. I knew Billy needed to know and Karen needed Billy there with her and their newborn child. *Oh, God, please let him call.*

He finally called, and I informed him what was happening. He went straight to the hospital to be with Karen and their son. His voice shook. "Mama, he is so small. I don't know what to do. I need him to live."

"Billy, listen to me. You have to trust God and believe he will live. Grandma said he would live. We are trusting in God that he will live. You, too, must believe that," I told him.

♦ ♦ ♦

The baby, William, gained weight, grew, and was full of life. Karen called, laughing and crying.

"Is everything OK with the baby?" I asked.

"Yes, he is 5 pounds today, and we can take him home!" she exclaimed.

It was a long road, but they were all finally coming home. Dawn and I had bought William a crib, and they set it up for the baby's homecoming. Billy was so protective of his new family. They had books for everything. Billy and Karen were talking about day care centers, high schools, and good colleges. "Slow down; he's just a baby," I said to them.

There was so much joy and laughter during those weeks. Billy was still working at night while Karen was at home caring for William. Karen let her man make all of the decisions. She always agreed with her Wise. Billy was in his glory. He was living in his grandma's house as a new father with a woman who loved him. Yes, life was good. By this time, he was renting his basement to his older brother, Walter, who was bringing in a little more money.

"Mama, why didn't you name me William?" he asked one day.

"Billy is short for William, and I liked Billy. You can always use your middle name," I said.

"Stop with the jokes, Mommy."

◆ ◆ ◆

Over the next year, Karen and Wise grew apart and separated. Billy was crushed. Karen moved back to Brooklyn with her mother and William. Over time, Billy tried to get his family back, but they remained separated. Billy and Karen talked and stayed close because they both loved William. Nothing could change the way they felt about their child. Billy was working, but he always felt it was never enough. "Mama, when you finish paying the bills, there isn't anything left. Even if I was working two jobs, it would not be enough," he said.

"Billy, stop talking like that," I told him. "Do not get into trouble."

The Runaway

Dawn ran away to Billy's house. Billy was very protective of his little sister.

"Now, Mama, she just wants to go to school with black kids—kids who look like her. What's wrong with that?" He was trying to rescue his sister.

"What if you take her and she runs away again and we don't know where she is?" I asked.

"Trust me, Mama. I got the Essence. I got this."

I realized that he was right and decided to let her stay.

Who would have thought that we would reach this point—Billy saving his baby sister? I was so proud of my son. He was a man now, taking care of Dawn, and loving his role. I had to step back, or I could lose my daughter. She was at an age when she was determined. I knew Billy loved her and would keep her safe.

"Mommy, you have my word. Please trust me. It will be all right," Billy told me.

Dawn was calling him Wise now. The whole family was referring to him as Wise. I was still calling him Billy.

The Mistake

Billy was still trying to get fast money. One day, he came to Pennsylvania. I was surprised to see him. "What's up, son?" I asked.

"What's wrong with a son visiting his mother?" he replied.

Of course, I became suspicious. I remember saying, "Billy, you are an adult now; please don't get involved in any bully shit."

"Mama, I swear to God, I am just visiting. Is there anything wrong with that?" he asked again.

"No, son, there is nothing wrong with that—just please, nothing dumb."

Billy would drive from New York to Pennsylvania once or twice a week. I would make his favorite banana pudding. He would update me as to how his little sister was doing in school. It was a good situation for both of us, but in the back of my mind, I felt he was up to something. He would talk about Karen and William. For a time, it was great—seeing him more often. I finally convinced myself that New York was only 175 miles or so. Maybe I should learn to trust my son more.

His brother David worked at a nearby nursing home. They would often visit together and go out to eat. *Maybe this is not a bad thing. Maybe I need to chill out and stop thinking the worst.*

♦ ♦ ♦

A few months passed, and then my mother called me. "Barbara, you need to come over now!" She lived about a quarter of a mile from me. When I arrived at her house, I could see she had been crying and looked lost.

"What's going on? Is everyone OK? Please tell me no one died."

My mother said the FBI had been there earlier to question Billy's brother. It seemed that Billy was purchasing guns in Pennsylvania and selling them in New York. I could feel my heart beating fast. My God, I had left New York City and took my children to the small town of Berwick, Pennsylvania, to ensure that they would be spared the violence of street gangs, guns, and drive-bys.

It seemed that Billy and his brother had purchased the guns. His brother was involved with the purchase of two guns. Billy had bought over forty guns and sold them. I asked his brother, "How long did you know about this? Why did you not tell me? What were you thinking?" This was a nightmare. I had felt something was wrong. I just did not think it was something this bad. In the months to come, we stayed in prayer.

I called Billy while he was at work, driving the ambulance. He asked, "What's up, Mother? I am going to take Dawn with me to see William later…"

I cut him off. "Billy, listen to me. The FBI came to Grandma's house to question your brother."

I heard him breathing. "For real, Mommy? What did they want?" he asked.

"They showed Grandma and your brother pictures and said that you were gun trafficking from Pennsylvania to New York."

"Mama, what did Brother say?"

"I don't know what he said. All I know is what I am telling you," I said.

"Damn, Mommy. Damn. Let me call you back."

"OK," I said, "I'll wait for your call. Call me back. Love you."

"Love you, too, Mama."

A few minutes passed. Karen called. She was crying. "I told Wise not to do this, that he made enough money working. He would not listen. I'm scared of what's going to happen. Wise could go to jail. I just wish he had not done this."

"Karen, we will survive this," I assured her. "The FBI said they weren't sure if Billy's brother would go to jail, but he said Billy would because he bought most of the guns and they were put in the wrong hands. He said so far no one was killed, but someone had been shot and another robbed with the guns." While explaining to Karen what had happened, I realized how much trouble my son was in.

I remember praying and asking, "How can this be happening?" All I could think of were the guns. Billy had assured me he was not involved in drugs. He became outraged when I was suspicious and asked, "Billy, are you involved in drugs?"

"Mommy, everyone thinks that black people sell drugs—not my own mama, too. I promise you I don't use drugs. I don't sell drugs." Well, Lord, he was not lying about that, but guns…Lord, I moved to the woods. How could this be happening? *Lord, where do we go from here?* Billy had sold over forty guns. Thank God no one was killed. Billy started realizing what could happen because of his actions. He realized that he would be taken away for a while. He would be locked away from his family—his son—and it could be a long time. He knew he would face this, and he knew that it would affect the rest of his life. His biggest fear was losing William.

♦ ♦ ♦

Billy called one night, and his voice cracked. "Mommy, listen to me. You have been a good mother. Please don't blame yourself for anything. This was all me. Mommy, no matter what happens, take care of William. Call Karen. Mommy, I messed up."

Lord, I don't like what he's done. God, I pray that he comes through this. I am his mother, and under those mistakes, I love him. I would stand by him through it this time. *We will get through this as a family. We will face it together, head on.*

"Mommy, are you mad?" Billy asked.

"Disappointed, not mad," I answered.

"Mom, I am sorry. I was just trying to make some money. I know it was not right. This time, I really messed up."

The Indictment

Billy was indicted for gun trafficking. The trial took about a year. I know he had never been separated from the family. He had never been around the kind of people he would encounter in jail. Fear began to fill my mind and heart. I remember hearing a TV preacher say, "God did not give us the spirit of fear. If you are in fear, you are in disbelief." I decided that morning to trust God and believe that Billy would come through this darkness intact.

William needed his dad. Billy needed William. *Please, God, let the judge understand. Don't let him spend all of his young years behind bars. Far too many young people lose so many years for stupid mistakes. Spare my child, Lord.*

Billy was given a legal lawyer from the Poconos. He would meet the lawyer at a local Denny's restaurant. "Mama, the fat bastard eats like a pig. I ask him about my case, and he orders more coffee. He's always telling me how much money his clients pay. Mommy, what the hell?"

I said to him, "Billy, when you decide to live a life of crime, always save for legal fees."

"Now my own mama is coming with jokes?"

I said, "Just keep praying no one is killed with those guns."

◆ ◆ ◆

During the time he was out on probation, my mother sold her home in New York. Billy moved to a small apartment in Brooklyn. Dawn called me one day from her dad's home in New York. "Mama, I went to see Billy. He was not eating and looked bad."

My mother and I drove to New York. My mom reached out her hand. "Son, it's time to come home. We will wait together until you go in."

His eyes were red. He smiled. "Grandma, I am not going to argue with grown folks." He put his stuff in the van, and we went back to Pennsylvania.

We waited on the judge's decision together as a family. We had never been closer. We prayed a lot. Billy did not talk much about going to prison, but I knew it was weighing heavily on his mind. He picked up his role as a big brother. He talked to his younger brother, Warren. Billy would use himself as an example on how precious from was. "Warren, this is my fault. No one put a gun to my head. I am losing my freedom for dumb shit. Don't make the same dumb mistakes I did. Keep your ass in school."

Billy did not have any money. What he had, he gave to Karen. Antoine and I had adopted three girls. We were still raising children. "Son, I cannot afford to pay attorney fees."

"Mother, I got myself into this mess. Please don't you and Antoine try to fix this situation. This is my mess. All I ask is that you and Grandma pray." And pray we did.

Billy again met with his attorney. "Mommy, that man has my future in his hands, and he never knows anything about the case. I think while buying his lunch, I am paying him too much. Damn, damn." We both laughed. Sometimes laughter is the best medicine.

◆ ◆ ◆

Time went on, and the trial came to an end. We waited for the sentencing. He got three-and-a-half years. The judge had been kind. William was still young, and he would not notice his dad being away. Billy had a few months before he had to turn himself in. He spent a lot of his time with William. He and his siblings started to get closer. He loved his grandma. Over the next few weeks, the little brother and sister he was so jealous of became his biggest supporters.

Billy had made a life-changing mistake. He would serve time in federal prison. He faced it like a man. He took responsibility for his actions. He was becoming a man I could respect in spite of what we were facing.

Billy loved to talk. He would go into detail. Our time was up; he had to turn himself in. We drove to the federal courthouse in Williamsport. Dawn,

Warren, and Billy talked and teased each other all the way there. I drove the car. I could not help thinking how my three youngest children loved each other. We were a family. We were closer at this time than ever before. *I won't cry or scream.* My son would be gone for three-and-a-half years.

God, please give me the strength to go through these next few years, the next few hours. A mother never gets accustomed to one of her children being taken away. I knew in my heart he had to go. The judge had been fair.

The Separation

We pulled up in front of the courthouse. We said our good-byes in the car. When he got to the court stairs, he turned around and looked at us with a big smile. Then, he went up the stairs to face the next few years. By this time, we were all crying. We had tried to be strong, but seeing him on the stairs broke my heart. I had worked hard all my life, running from crime—hiding, if you will—and still, my son was going to jail. *Billy is alive, and for that I am thankful. We do everything as a family, and this family shall survive this difficult time. This too shall pass.*

After a few days, Billy wrote to say they were moving him to Brooklyn, New York. Billy wrote, *Mama, these white guys are crazy. They get upset and bent out of shape when the COs call them names or yell at them. That shit makes me feel right at home. I spent time with Uncle Curtis, thank God; I know that's how it is in real life. Maybe the COs should refer to them as sir!*

He was soon transferred to Brooklyn. I was working night shift and decided to write to him while I was at work. I would write every night. We were starting to know each other in a different way. We were getting closer. We had code names for everyone. I had asked him if he was safe and if he was being treated with diligence. He said, "Mama, I am in a federal penitentiary, aka jail. No one messes with me. I can do this. I don't need my mama worrying about me. Think of it as free room and board. Keep your letters coming. I was in the hold reading your letter about Mr. Antoine, aka Locks. I busted out laughing. The CO asked if I was crazy. Mama, just keep those letters coming."

I looked forward to writing and to receiving his letters. In letters, I asked Billy if he needed money in his conversary. He wrote, *Mama, My conversary is quite fat, and I have been able to give Karen a little something-something.*

Wise Choice

My alarm went *off*. What was he up to now? Hell, Billy's in jail. In my next letter, I wrote, *Billy, my child, I want you to walk the straight and narrow, follow the rules, stay out of the hole. You don't want to do something that will give you more time.*

God, please help my son follow the rules.

Billy wrote back, *Mommy, please don't worry. I love you. I got to make it do what it do.*

I remember thinking, *What does that mean? Will he or won't he do the right thing? What can he do? After all, he is in jail.*

I found out a few weeks later that he and his sister, his partner in crime, were operating a cigarette ring.

Damn, I had just written him to walk the straight and narrow. *How hard could this be?*

Billy called one day. "Mama, I got your letter; now hear me. I have a son who needs clothes, shoes, and food. I am his father. This is my responsibility. Karen needs money. As a man, I need to provide for my son. Mama, I love you. Now, Mama, I got to make it do what it do. I love you. Can you pray I don't get caught?" We both laughed.

I remember trying to pray on this, but how? *Lord God, please protect all that is involved.* Later, I heard the business expanded into liquor. Someone would place the packages in foil and put them in mop buckets and garbage cans near the kitchen where inmates would retrieve them. Somehow, the families would Western Union the money to his sister, who would inform Billy the families received the packages. Then he would distribute the stuff. Now I was praying that my daughter did not get involved. She never explained to me how the process worked. I got it by word of mouth and put a lot of it together in my mind. *Lord, please God, do not let this cause him more problems in the future.*

Walter picked me up one Mother's Day. He said, "Mama, David and I are going to see Billy."

"It's time for Billy to see his mother," I said. I rode with them. It had been almost two years. When he came downstairs, my eyes filled with tears. He looked well. Of course, he was joking. "When the CO told me my mother was downstairs, I thought he was lying. Mama, is that you?"

"Yes!" I exclaimed.

This was my third son. I missed him so much. Writing is one thing, but being able to hug and kiss your son is so much more rewarding. It had been some time, but he was alive. I did not ask anything about his business. I just told him I was praying for him and that I loved him. I just turned it over to God.

◆ ◆ ◆

We went through the next few months. Billy kept his business running. He was able to save a few thousand dollars. He would be released to a halfway house in Scranton, Pennsylvania. He got a job at a nearby warehouse, working ten-hour days. He could take a bus to work.

"Mama, I am thankful for the job, but it's no money. By the time I give to Karen for William…there ain't shit left."

"Son, where are you going with this type of talk?" I asked. "Please remember that you are on parole. You don't want to go back to jail."

"Mama, only you think like that. I am not talking about selling drugs or guns. I am talking about clothes, Mama. Mama, clothes. The kids up here buy that shit; they will pay real money to look like someone from the hood, for real. I have to make it do what I do for real."

We went to lunch. After lunch, he went back to his halfway house. When his parole was over, Billy moved to Hazelton in the same building as his sister, Dawn.

Truck Driving

After about a year, he talked to his uncle Donald, who was a truck driver. They started driving tractor-trailers together. Uncle Donald was his trainer. He liked driving and often said he could make enough to live on. After being on the road for about a year, he was hired with a company that got him home nightly. He was very happy about that. "Mama, when I give Karen William's money, there's something left for a brother. You know, a little something-something."

"Boy, are you going to walk the straight and narrow?" I asked.

"Mama, I am never going back to jail," he said.

"Baby, Mommy will hold you to that, OK?"

"Mama, this you can take to the bank and cash." We both laughed.

◆ ◆ ◆

After about a year, Billy moved to White Hall, Pennsylvania. He got a truck-driving job there. He was home every day and worked nights. He loved being able to come home every day. He rented a nice twobedroom apartment. He was making $1,100 a week. "Mama, I did not bring this much home biweekly! Now I get it every week—a little something-something. I go into New York and New Jersey late at night. No traffic. Mama, I love this job. Thank God Uncle Donald convinced me to drive," he said. He had been on the road for nine months. For the first time, I did not feel like he was up to something.

Dawn would go see Billy. I no longer wondered if they were partners in crime. Billy would often tease me. "Mama, I cannot believe you got that man cutting three acres of grass with a push mower. Mama, you oughta quit." He laughed. "Mama, that's crazy." He was happy. "Mama, I wish I knew you could make this much money driving truck. I never would have messed with that other stuff." I felt my son was finally starting to learn.

NaCola Enters Our Lives

One day, Billy called and said, "Mommy, I met this woman on the computer. Her name is NaCola. She is a teacher. She has a son. She lives on the West Coast in LA."

A few weeks passed. "Mommy, remember I told you I met this lady on the computer?"

I asked, "Billy, are you talking about the schoolteacher?"

"You remember ? You were listening?"

"Yes. What about her?"

He began to explain. "Well, NaCola and her son are coming over for a visit."

A week passed. Billy called me. "Mama, I like this girl, but she lies about everything. Damn, Mama, she said she had twelve thousand dollars saved. That was a lie. She doesn't have any money. She doesn't have her own place. She lives with her sister, nephew, mother, and son in a two-bedroom apartment. I am sending her ass back to LA."

"Billy, do you like this girl?" I asked.

"Yes, but she lies about everything. Damn."

A few days later, I called Billy. "Did NaCola go back to LA?"

"No, we are working through some things. Her son, Anthony, is a pain in the ass. He tries not to listen to his mother. I had to tell him there was only one man in this house and that he would listen to his mother. Mama, I like this woman. It's just that she lies about everything. She did not have any money," he said again.

"Billy, you make good money. You do not need her money," I explained to him.

"That is true. It's just the lies that concern me. She is a teacher, and it's the little shit."

"Billy, she wanted to look good," I told him. "Everyone does that kind of thing."

"I guess you're right."

William was visiting on weekends. I asked how William was with Anthony and NaCola. "They are doing all right together, and William seems to like NaCola," Billy said. They were going to buy bunk beds for Anthony's room to make a place for William to sleep when he was there. Karen was starting to let William spend more time with Billy. "Mama, William called me one night and said he loved NaCola." I did not say anything. "Mama, say something. What's wrong with him loving NaCola?" Billy asked.

"How did Karen react to that?" I asked.

"Well, Karen talked to NaCola and was not upset. Karen and NaCola are becoming friends."

♦ ♦ ♦

William was spending more time with Billy. Billy, NaCola, and the boys were starting to look like a family. I believe that Karen must have known that her time was short, and she was trying to find a loving home for William. She was looking for another woman to take her place. I believe God, the Holy Spirit, sometimes gives us a glimpse of the future. Karen was encouraging William to spend more time with Billy and NaCola. It was time for William to know this man, who from birth had always found a way to provide for him, sometimes at great cost. Karen had suffered from sickle-cell all her life. She always seemed to be in pain and was in and out of the hospital her whole life.

God had given her William. They both almost died, but he grew. They both lived. William was Karen's joy. She was so happy when talking about him. I remember asking if he was a lot of trouble to her. Karen's eyes lit up. A big smile spread across her face. She said, "Trouble? Barbara,

Mrs Barbara Jean Obas

please listen to me. William is my light, my job. He's why my heart beats." I remember thinking how much contentment she had with her son. Despite the other problems she faced, it was not like Karen to let William go anywhere for a week.

Karen's Passing

One night, I was driving to Dawn's house in Hazelton when Billy called. He was screaming. I asked, "Son, did you have an accident?"

"No, Mommy. Karen is dead."

I pulled over. "What did you say, son?"

"Mommy, Karen died. NaCola called me. I just got to work, and she said, 'Billy, come back home.' I explained that I was at work and asked her to just tell me. She said Karen died. I called Karen. It's true. Mommy, Karen is gone. How am I going to tell William?" he pleaded for an answer.

"Billy, are you going to New York?" I asked.

"No, Mother. William is at the house with NaCola. I am on my way home. What will I say? How can I tell my son that his mother…his mother… Mama, how can I tell him when I can hardly say it?"

"Billy, pray. Trust God to give you the right words. I don't know, but God knows. Keep praying. The words will come, and they will be the right ones. I will call Grandma, Antoine, and the rest of the family," I told Billy.

"OK, Mama, I am at the house."

I got to Dawn's house. She was crying. "Mama, I cannot believe Karen is dead. Mama, I wish over the years we had gotten close. Now it's too late," she sobbed.

Dawn regretted that time had run out. When I got back home, I called Billy. He had told William. I could hear him crying in the background. I talked to Billy. He was also crying. Although they had been separated for many years, they both loved William. They loved each other because of William.

During this time, NaCola seemed very supportive and sensitive to what was going on with Billy and William. NaCola helped Billy work through his grief. Billy and I were to drive to New York for Karen's funeral with NaCola and Anthony. NaCola thought Billy and I needed this time alone, that he and I needed some space to talk. NaCola was very understanding and prayed for the family. Throughout the trip to New York, I remember telling Billy how thoughtful she had been throughout the ordeal.

"She has helped me a lot during this time. I would have been lost had she not been here," Billy said.

Billy and I had a lot of time to talk, but we were both just thinking about William. My biggest fear was that this would be the night...the night that this entire whirlwind would finally be real to him.

I feared how he would respond to seeing his mother's body. Billy and I left White Hall early to get to the funeral home early. We wanted to be there when William arrived. Karen's dad was there. His eyes were red. I could see a grown man, a father, trying to understand. I could feel his grief. He spoke to Billy and me as we walked up to the open coffin. I could see it was Karen. The pain was evident on her face. Karen. I remembered her beautiful smile, her warm voice. She was always reassuring me that William was all right. None of the rest of the family had arrived yet. I could see the pain on my son's face. A pain I had never seen before. He didn't talk much.

The rest of Karen's family began to arrive. Billy called Kevin, Karen's brother. Billy told him we were there waiting. They soon arrived with William. I watched him. I prayed that he would get through this. I know how close they were, just the two of them. He was her life, her joy. Those words kept going through my head. Somehow, we got to the viewing. William seemed to be all right. I believe Karen's spirit carried him through. My heart ached for Karen's mother. I remember thinking, *How do you bury your child? Lord, may I never experience this pain.* Karen was gone, her body before us. I realized at this moment how much time I had missed. Karen had gone home. Her beautiful smile, her joy. Gone.

After the services, I asked Billy if we could go by the house.

"Mama, I just want to go home," Billy said.

We said good-bye to William and went to the car. Billy didn't talk until we go into Pennsylvania.

"Mama, I still cannot believe she is gone. She never did anything bad to anyone. Why Karen, William's mother?"

I listened to my son, and then I told him, "Karen is with God."

"Mommy, William needs her here."

"Billy, I love you," I told him.

"I love you, too, Mommy. This is so unfair."

He called NaCola and told her we were almost back to the apartment. She had some food ready when we got back. I slept overnight. The next morning, we were to go to the burial. When I woke up, Billy had already left. NaCola said he wanted to be by himself. So I had breakfast and went back home. My son and grandson would go through this together. *Lord, I trust in you,* I prayed as I drove home. My thoughts were in New York with my son.

William had lost his mother, and I just could not help thinking about the timing. Billy was out of jail, and he had found a job where he could be home daily. He had a nice lady. Karen must have felt that she couldn't let go until Billy had made it on his own. Now Billy was ready to love and care for William. Maybe she thought the time was right. Only God knows. We may not always understand it, but we must accept it.

The next few weeks were difficult, but time moves on, regardless of life's misfortunes. We kept moving forward. I called Billy and asked how William was doing. I called Beverly, William's grandmother, to check on William and the family. I knew this was a pain that would remain with them forever. I prayed and tried to comfort them. I didn't know what to say. Most of the time, I just listened.

♦ ♦ ♦

A few weeks later, I had to call my son. "Billy, when will you be bringing William home?" I asked.

"Mama, I will be taking him this summer after school is finished. We are looking for a larger apartment so William can have his own room. I want to give him time to adjust to moving with us. He has always been with Karen's family. He is only with us on weekends. This will be a transition, but he will be here to live," Billy explained.

"OK, that's good to hear."

"Mama, it's time for you to step up. You need to visit and call him. Mama, you need to get to know your grandson."

"I will do my part. I am just a grandmother. You are his father," I told Billy.

"He needs you, Mama. He needs you, too."

"OK, son, I hear you, and I am here. I am not going anywhere, trust that."

Billy replied, "OK, Mommy."

Billy and NaCola found a larger apartment not far from the first one. Billy was excited.

"Mama, too many nonworking people are moving in this place. If you get ten days behind on your rent, you get kicked out. So I know working people live here. The master bedroom has its own bathroom. I know this is the right move. I am going to get William's stuff before he moves in," Billy told me over the phone.

"Everything sounds great, son." My son was now a family man, planning a future for his new family.

Billy called a few nights later. "Mama, NaCola just wants to spend money. I told her we have to save. It is not how much you spend, but how much you save. Mama, how much do you have saved?"

"Boy, it's not about me," I said.

"OK, Mama."

A New Life

William had lived with his mother and her family from a very early age. They were a close family. This move would be a big transition for him. It was important for Billy to keep them in William's life. They were Karen's family. William's new environment included a new stepbrother, mother figure, school, and apartment. Love would make all of these new changes possible. Once William moved in with his dad, it was decided he would go to Brooklyn on some weekends to spend time with Karen's family. Karen's brother, Kevin, and Billy shared the transportation to and from Brooklyn. Billy was very happy and proud to have his son with him. Billy was also starting to develop a relationship with Anthony. This was starting to look like a young family.

A few weeks passed since William had moved in. Billy called late one night. "Mommy, can you talk?"

"Yes, son, I am at work finishing my paperwork. What's up?" I asked.

"Mommy, we just got past Karen's death…" he stopped talking.

"What's wrong, son?"

"Mommy, NaCola is pregnant."

"Hot damn, that's good news! You scared me. Hell, that's great news!" I said excitedly.

"Mommy, I was thinking by the time I was forty-five, all the kids would be grown. A baby is starting all over again."

"Billy, this is good news," I told him. "Just think, a baby—it would seal the family. A baby would make William and Anthony big brothers. Think of how cute this little guy or girl will be."

"Mama, babies cost money. They cry all night."

"OK, it's a good thing you work nights," I said jokingly.

"Very funny, Mama. You always are making jokes."

"Billy, you are going to be very happy. Just wait until you hold the baby. They bring a lot of joy."

"Joy?" he questioned. "Hell, they cost a lot of money, Mommy."

NaCola wanted a girl. Billy wanted a boy. They each wanted to name the baby, but both had very different name choices. They were happy about the newest family member. One night, Billy said, "Mommy, I missed a lot of William's baby moments, like his first steps and his first word. I am going to enjoy this. I will be almost fifty-five when this baby is grown. That's crazy."

I chuckled a little. "Children keep life interesting."

"I guess. If you say so."

♦ ♦ ♦

NaCola's mother came to visit a few months before the baby was born. Billy brought his family to my house. Billy and the boys went swimming in my mom's pool. I got a chance to pat NaCola's tummy while Mom and the rest of the females watched the boys play with floats in the pool. NaCola told us she was having a boy. She and Billy still had not chosen a name, but the entire family was very happy. These were good days, indeed.

The time flew by, and one morning, Billy called. "Mama, NaCola is going to the hospital. I need to you come to the house to stay with William and Anthony. I missed William's birth; I don't want to make that mistake again. I don't want to miss a minute."

"You sound nervous. This will be fine; everything will be just fine," I said, trying to calm him.

"We are in the new apartment. Don't get lost. See you soon."

When I got to the apartment, William and Anthony were playing games in their room. I asked them if they were excited about the new baby. Anthony was excited. He told me how he would hold the baby and help him. He was a little nervous and wanted to meet him. William, on the other hand, told me that the baby stuff was in his closet. He showed me the closet and explained that it took up most of his space. He was somewhat reserved about the arrival. I remember thinking that this was truly a family.

The next morning, the boys went off to school. I got dressed and waited for Billy and NaCola to bring my newest grandson home. His name was Billy Raphael Brewster Jr., aka BJ. This was just the best day! Billy brought the baby upstairs first. Then he went down to help NaCola up. NaCola looked tired, as she should after a delivery. BJ was beautiful. My son talked for a few minutes. I could see that he was looking for a way to be with NaCola and BJ alone before the boys were to come home.

Billy walked me to my car. I had to work that night, but I still had a few hours to get home and sleep. I said good-bye and went home. I talked to Billy the next day. He was very happy. He was proud of his family. There seemed to be so much love in their home. Billy loved NaCola. She loved him. She helped the boys with their homework, cooked, and started teaching Billy about the Bible. One night, Billy called and said, "Mama, I feel happy for the first time in my life. I feel happy!"

"Billy, my son, that's what a family will do for a man."

A few nights later, he called again. "Mama, do you think Grandma would mind if we had Thanksgiving at our house? BJ is less than a month old, and I want to have it at my house."

"I will talk to Granny," I said. "I am sure that will be OK."

♦ ♦ ♦

We went to Billy's for Thanksgiving. We took along side dishes. William was at the Vassels's home in New York. Those in attendance at our Thanksgiving included Grandma; my cousin Naomi; Dawn Essence; my oldest son, Walter; NaCola's mom; and, of course, the newest little family member, BJ. The guys were in the bedroom, watching the football game, while the ladies spent time in the living room, admiring the baby.

Billy was waiting for Black Friday. He was going to buy his sixty-inch TV. He looked like the child I remembered at Christmas, anxiously waiting for the night to pass to see the gifts in the morning.

The next day, he called. "Mama, I got it!" He was laughing.

I started teasing, "What did you get, my son?"

"A sixty-inch TV. It was on sale, and now it's in my car."

Then I started to joke. "William, Anthony and Billy wanted me to ask you if they could play games on the new TV."

"Mama, stop joking. This is for the man of the house."

Jokingly, I asked, "Which one? There are four."

"No, Mama, there is one man and three boys. Please know that the man is the one that works and pays the bills up in here. One man, Mama."

"OK, son. I get the point."

A few nights passed. Billy called. I was on my way to work and feeling playful. I answered my phone and said, "What's up, Wise B. God?"

"Mommy, what did you say?"

Again, I joked, "What's up, Wise?"

He said, "My name is Billy Raphael Brewster."

I could not speak. My child had emerged into manhood.

"Mommy, the things I used to do, I don't do anymore. That was another time. That street shit—I don't bring it into my house. I have a family. Mama, there was a time when I would drink a pint of liquor at two in the morning. I don't do that shit anymore. And Mama, I am happy. I just want to make this work."

"I understand, son," I said, shocked.

"Mama, I bought insurance on everyone in the family. Don't want the children or NaCola to suffer if anything were to happen to me. You know, I drive a truck. Mama, I am going to adopt Anthony after NaCola and I are married. I want him to have my last name," he said.

"Billy, that's great news!"

A few weeks passed, and Billy called again. "BJ keeps NaCola up at night. She is so uptight. We need a vacation. Mama, I work hard all the time. I am going to use my vacation time to go on vacation. NaCola can use some time away from BJ. She needs some rest. Mama, I am thinking about a cruise. Just one week."

Wise Choice

Billy said NaCola was going to ask her mother, Viv, to take care of BJ. Billy and NaCola looked up different cruises on the Internet. He was excited. I had taken my family on a cruise when the boys were younger. Billy said he often thought about those days. He said, "Mama, I remember that. I loved that. I want to make memories like that with my family."

"You will, my son. You will have many memories throughout the years," I said.

"Yes, we will indeed."

A few nights passed. Billy called. I was off that night and watching TV. "Mama, I am going to ask NaCola to marry me. I already picked out the ring."

I asked, "What does the ring look like?"

He said, "The diamond is so big. I put it in my drawer until I got home." He was laughing.

"Son, don't forget to call me when she says yes," I said.

"Mama, of course she will say yes."

"Just call when she does."

The next morning, they called. They were so happy and excited. NaCola told me that my son got down on both knees. She said yes. They would marry after their vacation.

Billy called. "Mama, NaCola's mom just got married and is unable to babysit. We need a babysitter for your grandson. Do you think you can get some time off?"

"When are you guys going?" I asked.

"First week in July. The first through the seventh."

"Rough week, but I will ask my supervisor," I said.

"Mama, please make it do what it do," Billy said to me.

"I will try. Regardless, I will arrange something."

"Mama, NaCola wants you to watch the baby at our house so the baby is comfortable with his surroundings."

"OK, son, let's see if I can get this time off."

My supervisor rearranged some things, and I was able to take off work for their vacation. The vacation was saved. They texted me pictures of BJ. NaCola was unsure about leaving him. She wanted to go on vacation, but at the same time, she did not want to leave her baby. He was breastfed. I told her to transition BJ to a bottle since she would not be home to supply what he needed. NaCola laughed. "I am trying, but he insists on breastfeeding."

"Try harder because he needs to use the bottle," I said.

NaCola did not want to leave the baby, but she needed a vacation. Billy called me one night and said, "Mama, I don't care if she goes or not; my boys and I will be on that ship." He was laughing. This would be the first family vacation. "Mom, do you know where we can buy a cheap luggage set?"

"Billy, watch the Sunday papers. There are usually good sales there."

He called again. "Mama, I don't remember you and Richard going through all of this packing for your vacation."

"Believe me, it was the same," I assured him.

This was the first time William would vacation with his father. He had vacationed with Karen's family at Disney World. Now he would get to know his dad in a different light. The boys were ready for the trip.

The Vacation

I stayed at their house the night before their departure so they could get an early start. The alarm went off at 6:00 a.m. sharp. The suitcases were already packed. I heard someone in the shower. There was movement in the house, and I was surprised to see that the boys were getting dressed. Billy was still sleeping, and NaCola was feeding BJ. There was excitement in the air! NaCola brought BJ out to me so she could start getting ready.

Billy came out, and I could tell he was still sleepy. "Mama, I am going to take a shower. We are going to get out of here soon. It's a two-hour drive."

NaCola showed me where to find all of BJ's necessities. She made a list of all of his likes and dislikes on a chalkboard. I remember thinking, *What a fuss muffin.* I was happy to know BJ was loved.

The boys started packing the car. NaCola was fussing over BJ and giving me last-minute details on his TV schedule. *Yo Gabba Gabba* was his favorite show. Then she started discussing his different strollers and when to use each. NaCola wanted to go on vacation, but she was having a difficult time leaving her baby.

Everything was packed in the car and ready to go. NaCola kissed BJ and said good-bye. Three minutes later, she was back upstairs because she said she forgot something. This repeated two more times. I finally saw the car moving. "BJ, I do believe they have left," I told him. He was sound asleep, unaware of family being away. NaCola started texting me. She seemed to be happy and nervous at the same time. This baby was very lucky to get so much attention.

They arrived at the ship. NaCola texted me pictures. There was a picture of Billy and NaCola standing in front of the ship. They looked like children next to the big vessel. Billy looked so happy. The boys were taking pictures. I, on the other hand, had plenty of plans for my tiny lad, BJ. Grandma would get some sugar from that man.

BJ and I had a wonderful week. It was over too soon. During the week, NaCola called. "I miss my baby. How are things going?"

"BJ's fine. Where are you?" I asked.

"Freeport."

I could hear Billy say in the background. "My mama's got this. Come on."

"Is he drinking well from the cup?" she asked.

"NaCola, BJ is with my mama; say good-bye."

◆ ◆ ◆

The seven days went by fast. They called when the ship was docked and said they would be home in a few hours. NaCola wanted to hold her baby. When they got home, they all looked very tired, but Billy had a big smile on his face.

"Did you have a good time?" I asked.

"Mama, it was good. I gave extra tips."

NaCola, who was now holding BJ, said, "I want to start saving for next year. It was beautiful, but I missed my baby."

I told Billy I wanted to take the bus home, so he drove me to the bus stop. "Mommy, it was so beautiful. Ships are a lot different since we were on a cruise. It was absolutely beautiful. Next week, NaCola has some job interviews. Her cousin is coming to babysit BJ," he explained to me on the car ride.

"That's good news," I said.

Billy was excited and tired, but he had to return to work that night. I wanted to get to my bus so he could get a few hours of sleep. The bus arrived, and Billy got out of the car, fussing. "Mama, you work hard. You need to buy yourself a decent car."

"I will, son."

A few days passed. NaCola texted pictures of BJ. Billy called me on his way to work. All was good in the world. One morning when driving home, I found myself singing old hymns. *What a friend we have in Jesus, just a closer walk with thee,* I found myself praying. I had a sense of sadness. I called my cousin. She said it was a sign of death. My first thoughts were of the oldest members of the family. My aunt Mamie and my mother were in their eighties. I remember praying, *Lord, bless them and keep them.*

One night, my daughter called. She was crying. "Mama, I dreamed Billy died." I had talked to Billy earlier, so I reassured Dawn that when we dream of a man, it's really a woman that the man represents. Life is the opposite of what we dream.

After she hung up, I called Billy. "Where are you?"

He said, "I am in the yard at the job, about to go home. I'm tired." I did not tell him of Dawn's dream because he was worried about Grandma.

Now, I know that God speaks to us through the Holy Spirit and sometimes he uses dreams to speak to us. He gives us little signs along the way. I missed every one of them. I thanked God for my life and all the wonderful things he had done in my life: my mother, husband, children, grandchildren, and sound mind. God would always be my provider. I was sure of this.

Mama, Please Don't Be Late!

One Week before the Wedding

Billy called. "Mama, make sure you get work off the night before the wedding. It's going to be a morning service. I know how you like to be late. Bring Grandma and David. Please, please be on time."

Two Nights before the Wedding

"Mama, I am just checking. Do you have off on Friday?" Billy asked.
"Yes, son."
"Please don't try to work half of your shift. Did you get your hair done?"
"Yes, son."
Billy was full of questions. "Is Grandma riding with you? We are leaving the apartment at eight thirty in the morning. If you are not here, I will be sure to tell you how great it was."
I then asked, "Billy, did NaCola get the pots?"
"Mama, don't worry about the pots. Just be on time."
"Billy, the week I spent at your house, I noticed that you need pots."
Billy replied, "Mama, did you call me to talk about pots? Mama, the pictures at Grandpa's house in the silver frame with my Pops and all of us together...I want that for our wedding present."
"OK, son. David is coming, too," I said.
"Please don't let him end up with that picture." David was famous for stealing pictures.
"Billy, I will put your picture in the trunk of my new car. It's yours," I said, trying to calm him.
"OK, Mama, that's your word."

The Night before the Wedding

"Mama, what are you doing? Trying to get one more hour of sleep before getting up?" Billy asked.

"Hey, Billy, I told you I would call you back," I said.

"Mama, you need to stop working nights. It's not good for your health." He sounded concerned.

"I know, son, but I have to work. Look who's talking; you drive at night."

"Mama, I am saving to buy a truck. I want to start my own business where I will make a lot more money. It will be great! Mama, NaCola will be working soon. Remember, it's not about how much you spend; it's how much you save. Trust that. When you used to tell me you did not have any money, I didn't understand why. I was starting to think you were on the pipe." He broke out laughing.

"The pipe, son? Go ahead, just quit. Billy, times are hard. I am going to start saving soon," I said.

"OK, Mama. Mama, you aren't going to believe this. NaCola asked her niece that is here to be her matron of honor, and at the last minute, she changed her mind. Do you think Dawn would do it?" Billy asked.

"Tell NaCola to ask Dawn," I said.

"Mom, would you ask her?"

After a pause, I agreed. "Yes, I will, because you know how Dawn likes to show off her stuff."

The next day, I asked Dawn. She said she would call NaCola to see what color dress she needed. Billy was happy.

The night before the wedding, Billy called. "Mama, I for one will be glad when we are married. This wedding stuff is crazy. It started out just you, Grandma, NaCola's mother, and her new stepdad. Every day, it gets bigger. Cousin Nick, Uncle Donald, three of NaCola's friends, David… Mama, I got to feed all these people." He started laughing. "Damn, the preacher is bringing more folks. Maybe I should ask the restaurant to give everyone their own bill," he added, still laughing.

"Billy, weddings cost money, and you said you were saving…"

The Wedding

"Mama, tomorrow morning, be at my house by eight fifteen. Now, I know you will be late."

"Billy, I have the night off. We will be there," I assured him.

"NaCola is driving me crazy. I wish we had not told anyone. She argues about everything. We should have gone to the justice of the peace like you and Antoine. It would have been cheaper, too," he said.

"Billy, this is an exciting day for the bride. She wants everything to be just right, and I am sure she is nervous, too. Believe it or not, this is a really big day for a woman. The bride needs everything to be perfect," I explained to him.

"I understand that. I am just tired of all the bullshit."

"Billy, are you sure this is what you want to do? This is the last time I will ask."

He paused. "Mother, this is the last time I will tell you…I love this woman. I am happy and I want to do right by this woman. She is also a good mother."

"OK, Billy, I will see you in the morning," I said.

"Mama, should I get a limo to pick up NaCola and Dawn in the morning? NaCola and her mother went to the beauty shop to get the works… hair and nails. That should calm her ass down," he said.

"I guess so."

"OK, tomorrow. I guess I should get ready for a wedding! See you and Grandma in the morning."

"You sure will, son."

"I hate to sound like a broken record, but Mama, please don't be late."

It was 5:00 a.m., *I can sleep for another half hour. Damn, 5:30 already? I better call Dawn so she can get going since she's the maid of honor.*

David answered. He said Dawn had just left. I called my mother and told her I would be leaving my house in about an hour. I picked up my mom at six-fifteen. I thought I should call David again and tell him that we were leaving the house.

"We are on our way. Was that Dawn's voice I just heard? You said she had left." I was puzzled.

"It's a long story." He began laughing. "I told her to leave."

"NaCola must be a wreck. Dawn's supposed to help her get dressed," I said to him.

"Calm down. Dawn is leaving now."

"OK, am I still picking you up?" I asked. "Damn, Billy will be upset if we are late!"

David said, "Calm down. Dawn is on her way. See you and Grandma when you get here."

"OK, son."

After picking David up, I told him to call Billy and tell him Dawn was on her way. After a few minutes, I asked, "David, did you call Billy?"

"Yes, Mama, but his line is busy. He's probably trying to call Dawn."

"David, this is so messed up. Dawn should almost be there," I said, worried.

"Weddings require a lot of phone calls. I am sure they are making last-minute arrangements," David said, trying to calm me.

We were getting close to the house and decided to stop at McDonald's to freshen up because I was sure both bathrooms at Billy's house would be occupied. I couldn't help but think that Billy was worried we had overslept. I tried calling him.

"David, you must be right. The line is still busy."

Then, we got a phone call from Dawn. She asked where we were. I asked Dawn where *she* was.

"Mama, you are not going to believe this, but somehow I got lost," she said.

"Damn, Dawn. We are pulling up in front of the building." I parked the car. "David, call your brother and tell him we are here. If he asks about Dawn, tell him what she said."

"Mama, the line is still busy." David replied.

Wait a minute. I just noticed police cars parked across the street. *I was here a whole week and never saw a police car.* The line was still busy.

"David, go tell Billy we are here and ask him if we should wait in the car or go upstairs."

"OK, Mommy."

David went upstairs. He soon came downstairs with a tall man. I saw David reach into his pocket. He appeared to be showing the man his ID.

"Mom, wait in the car, and let me see what is going on. When I got to the front door, the man identified himself as a Whitehall detective. I asked him if everything was OK, and he asked who I was."

I told the man that I was David's mother and that we were there to pick up my son, Billy, to take him to his wedding. The detective asked us to get back in the car and told us someone would be over to talk to us.

After getting back in the car, David said, "Mom, something is very wrong. They had yellow tape across Billy's door."

"My God, David, someone is hurt!"

Then David said, "The detective told me Billy was in the hospital."

"What hospital? We need to go to the hospital. Is Billy hurt?" I asked frantically.

"I don't know, Mom. He said to wait here. Someone will be over to talk to us."

Dawn was calling David because she was still lost. David stepped out of the car to speak to her.

I could see the strain on his face…something had happened. My mind was racing. *Where is Billy? Where are the children? Are Nick and his wife at the hospital? What is going on?*

An officer came to the car. "Can you follow me?" He wanted us to follow him to the police station. He took us through a single door, and we went upstairs to a conference room.

The News

They asked us to be seated. Cousin Nick and his wife were already there with William. We all hugged.

I was so relieved to see them. I asked Nick, "Where are Billy and NaCola?"

Before Nick could answer, a tall man walked into the room. He cleared his throat, told us who he was, and then said, "There is no nice way to say this. Mr. Billy Brewster is deceased."

My heart started beating fast. My mind was racing. I wanted to scream and cry. Maybe I had misunderstood what he had said. He was saying that my child, my son, my friend was…dead? Please, God, not dead.

I heard my son David ask, "What do you mean? What are you saying?"

I remember saying, "He's dead?" Then I asked, "Where are NaCola and the other children?"

"They are OK," he said.

"How can this be?" I asked. "I just talked to him last night, and he said that NaCola's mother and stepdad were at the door, so he would see us tomorrow. He said not to be late."

He cannot be dead. What could have happened? The police explained that NaCola was locked up. She was the one that killed Billy. Where were Anthony and BJ? It was like watching a bad movie. My mind could not comprehend what was occurring. I kept thinking that someone—anyone—would come in and say this was some kind of mistake. *This cannot be real. My son, my child, is gone. NaCola, the woman he was going to marry, killed him.*

Then an officer said that NaCola's mother wanted to talk to me about the children. I followed him to a room downstairs. Her mother came in. Her eyes were red and swollen.

I said, "She killed my baby."

She kept saying, "I am so sorry."

The Confession

Then, her mother said, "I wish NaCola would have just left." I was thinking, *Why would she leave?* Just a few hours ago, she was telling me she was so happy. Then, I realized she was trying to establish a reason for NaCola's actions. She was trying to protect her and was hoping through my confusion, I would buy into a lie. This was a mother's attempt to protect her child. Yet, my son was dead because of her daughter. There was nothing she could offer me. I began to feel very angry. I wanted to scream. She killed my baby!

She was still crying. "Barbara, NaCola wants me to raise BJ."

Was she crazy? She told me NaCola kept screaming, "Don't let them take my baby!" *Her baby is my grandson. Her son is Billy's baby. My God, what is happening?* I couldn't think. I remember the police officer saying that if we could not come to an understanding, he would have to go to Human Services. I could not see my grandson in foster care. I knew that she was his grandmother, too, and she would care for our grandchild. So, I gave her permission to take him back to her hotel. I thought I would take him later, after I talked to my family.

Dawn arrived at the police station. She had been crying. "Mom, she did not have to kill him. Why didn't she just leave?"

We hugged each other. "I know, baby. I know."

How do you comfort your child with this kind of hurt? This was supposed to be a happy day with people who loved each other. This was crazy. Billy had worked to take care of this woman for three years. She was BJ's mother. We were here for my son to marry this woman.

The police officer took us back upstairs to be with the rest of the family. The preacher, Pastor Derrick, who was supposed to marry Billy and NaCola, was there. He walked over to me, introduced himself, and asked if I was Billy's mother. I told him I was. I asked the pastor if my son had confessed hope in Christ. He smiled and said he had. I said, "God is good."

This evil act was not of God. God is good. I had to keep reminding myself of that to avoid losing my mind. Pastor Derrick said he had been studying with Billy and NaCola. He said before he could marry them, he had to teach them about God, about Jesus. He was confused as to what could have happened.

The coroner was also in the room. He bent down and said that Billy had been treated with respect. He said there were two stab wounds. One was not fatal. However, the other was a direct hit to his heart. They tried to revive him, but the damage was too severe. He said there were cuts on his arms too. Billy's body was at the coroner's office.

My mind was racing. He was dead, stabbed by NaCola. Somewhere in my mind, I could still hear my son saying, "Mama, I love this woman. I want to marry this woman." I looked around the room and saw David, Dawn, William, Nick and his wife, and my mother. I had to calm myself down. *If I fall apart, what will happen to the rest of the family? Lord, please take us through this. We have come through bad times in the past, and you always brought us through. So Jesus, I trust you now.*

Pastor Derrick must have been reading my mind because he said, "Let us pray. Lord, may we please pray this was a calming time."

We were standing in front of the police station. I don't remember coming down from upstairs, but I do remember those wonderful people praying with us. The police asked if the children needed clothes from the apartment because they were going to lock it up. We went to the apartment, and I looked around. Pictures were on the walls, the wedding dress was on the floor, and the baby stroller was by the door. The playpen was in front of the kitchen so BJ could watch his mom while she was cooking. They boys' rooms were a little messy with their TVs on the wall and computer games scattered about. A sign on the kitchen wall read "All because two people fell in love." This was a home—the home of my son and grandchildren. On the pantry door were NaCola's rules for the day, instructing the boys to put out the trash and wash the dishes.

Dear Lord, this was their home. It seemed as if nothing had changed. Dear God, everything had changed. Billy was dead, and NaCola was in jail. Did she think about the children? William had just lost his mother less than two years ago, and now he had lost his dad. He had watched the woman who was acting as his stepmother take his father's life. BJ was eight months old and needed his mother. *NaCola, did you think about your children?* My mind could not stop shouting, *What happened? How could something evil come into this house?* I continued to walk through the apartment. In the kitchen, there was a silver tray on the floor. I saw the knife set I had given them on Thanksgiving. Billy had called and asked me to bring the cutlery set for their first Thanksgiving at his house. That was our last Thanksgiving together. Did NaCola use one of those knives to kill my son?

I saw William putting clothes in a bag. He looked lost. He looked at me and said, "Grandma, I called Kevin and my grandma in New York. They are on their way."

I said, "William, I was going to take you with me."

"Grandma, I want to go back to New York."

I was not surprised. I knew that Karen's mother and brothers had raised William. He felt safe and loved by them. I know Karen's spirit was sending them. I thanked God that they were coming. I was hurting so bad that I may not have given William all the love and support he needed. This was his father and friend. He saw what happened. He was in so much pain, and I knew in my heart that the Vassels were closer to William than I was. The police soon told us that they had to secure the apartment, so we had to leave.

I looked at my mom. She looked so hurt. She had always said, "Barbara, Billy is the most down-to-earth son you have. I don't understand the others. Billy makes the most sense." She had lost her grandson. He always teased her and would say, "Grandma, you are a big girl."

The other family members looked hurt and confused. David kept saying, "What happened? What the hell happened?" Nick's eyes were red; his wife was trying to comfort him.

I called my sister-in-law in Chicago. She was laughing. "How are the newlyweds?" I tried to tell her what had happened, but I could not get the words out. She said, "Sis, I cannot understand you. What's wrong?"

"Billy is gone." I finally was able to murmur.

"Gone. Gone where?" she asked, confused. *God, how do you say he's dead?*

Nick took the phone and explained what had happened. She told the rest of the family in Chicago. The maintenance people were locking up the apartment. We went to our cars to wait on William's other family to arrive and take him back to New York. We went home and arranged Billy's funeral. The next few days were a daze. I was in a fog making the arrangements.

Saying Good-Bye

Since Billy was a working man, he had insurance. He did not have a beneficiary. He did not have anyone listed on his policy. We thought there would not be enough money but found that there was more than enough. The money would cover everything—not to mention the money from his company. Other drivers donated money to the family in his honor. I began to see God's hand in all of this. If you trust and believe, faith will bring you through. Thank God for his grace. My sister-in-law Angie gave us money, and my mother paid for the gravestone. Everything just came together.

After we buried Billy, my days were empty. I missed our nightly calls, his jokes, and the family updates. Every thought led me to Billy. I could not help but wonder, *What happened?* My nephew Nick tried to explain, but still I could not understand how something like this could happen. I started reading my Bible, trying to learn all I could to understand the Resurrection. God knows that the loss of a child has to be the hardest thing you can face in life.

I started therapy sessions. It helped to just talk to someone. It was too hard to talk to family about some of the feelings that often came in the wee hours of the morning. I wondered, *Did he suffer? Did he know that he was loved?* I loved him. God, I loved him. *Did he realize what was happening? Did anyone pray with him? Was he in pain?* I just kept replaying that night over and over in my head...what happened?

The local news kept the story running. NaCola continued to refuse to accept responsibility for her actions.

Scan in news article here.

NaCola refused a plea bargain. She went to trial, sparing the family nothing. NaCola was the only one who could answer my questions. She said she was upset and had had a bad day.

The following article was published on wfmz.com on September 12, 2012. It was authored by Katie Shank, web producer.

ALLENTOWN, Pa. -

A Lehigh County woman charged in the stabbing death of her fiancé on their wedding day is heading to trial.

A preliminary hearing was held Thursday for NaCola Franklin, and all charges were held for court.

Franklin killed her fiancé Billy Brewster inside their home in Whitehall Township last month, police said. It happened just hours before the couple was set to walk down the aisle, officials said.

Copyright 2012 WFMZ. All rights reserved. This material may not be published, broadcast, rewritten or redistributed.

© 2013 WFMZ-TV I 300 East Rock Road, Allentown, Pennsylvania

An argument broke out, and she called 911. The murder was caught on tape. She was screaming, "Put my baby down!" At some point Billy gave her BJ. She was screaming, "You are going to die tonight! Die! Die! I am going to kill you! Die!" Those were the last words Billy heard his bride-to-be say to him, instead of hearing, "I am sorry; I love you." God, please forgive me, she intended to kill him and she did.

NaCola killed Billy for her own reasons. We may never understand why. I thank God that I am a believer. The Bible says, "You can kill the body, but you cannot kill the soul." Billy, I know that your soul is with your father.

NaCola was found guilty of first-degree criminal homicide. She was sentenced to life in prison.

Somehow I can still hear Billy saying, "Momma, you and Grandma, please don't be late…"

The Family's Prepared Wisdom Statements

My last words to NaCola at her sentencing

At last, this can be about Billy R. Brewster, the young man's life you took. Billy had many plans for his future. He had started saving to buy a truck. He wanted to make more money to provide a good life for you and the children. At that time, we both worked nights. That's when he gave me updates on how you and the children were doing. I got to know you through our many phone conversations.

One night, the first red flag went off. Billy told me that your brother was released from prison. Billy said he wanted to come to Pennsylvania. I remember asking if he would live with you guys. "Don't be scared, Mom. NaCola won't let that happen because of the boys."

When William lost his mother, you seemed so kind and caring. Billy told me that William was calling you "Mom." I must say I was somewhat reserved, but Billy was happy. So I was happy for this new family.

Then you gave us BJ. I remember you wanted to name him Noah. Billy wanted a junior. In the end, we would have two Billys. I asked Billy about the children. He would tell me what the older boys were up to and would say, "As for BJ, he's on the tit."

Billy called when he had finished paying for the ring. "Mama, I am going to get on one knee." Later, you both called, laughing. You told me he got down on both knees.

Billy was aware of crime. He wanted his children to attend gang-free schools and live in a safe neighborhood. He was working long, hard hours to ensure that occurred. The danger that he worked so hard to protect his family from was at home, lying in his bed. You killed him because you knew he had been drinking. You took advantage of him. You showed no concern about the father of your sons, William, Anthony, or BJ. You knew that Billy was William's only living parent. The last words that William, Anthony, and BJ heard you say to their dad were, "You're going to die tonight!" Die. A mother killed a father with the children watching. In doing this, yes, you killed my son. However, you also took your own life. You will never see BJ go to daycare, go to his first day of kindergarten, play sports, graduate from high school…you will miss it all.

The second flag that rose was after you killed Billy, when your mother told me that she knew what I was going through because the police had killed your brother in LA during a bank robbery.

NaCola, my son was killed in his home. He worked, paid the bills, and took care of his family. Billy was killed by the woman he loved. Billy Brewster was a working man. You don't know how I feel. You have no idea what I am going through.

Conclusion

When I looked around the courtroom after the sentencing, I thanked God for giving us Billy for thirty-six years.

I thanked God for all our young people and my family.

We would start again with love.

The Bible teaches, "Love bare, believes, hopes. Love is suffering. Love cannot fail."

This family received the justice they deserved but at a very dear price.

I am trusting God.

If anyone reading this book is in a relationship that involves domestic violence, please seek help.

Let's stop the violence and protect families. Please think of your mothers and children who will have to go on without you.

Pastor Derrick has given me the peace I need to finish running this race. When my time is finished, I am assured that I will join Billy again.

I know that will be a glorious day!

So until then, my son, "Be good. I know you have to make it do what it do."

—Mother

The following article was published on lehighvalleylive.com on May 24, 2013, authored by Precious Petty.

Billy Brewster, killed by fiancé on wedding day, was hard-working, family man, cousin says

Billy Brewster was a hard-working family man who looked forward to spending the rest of his life with **NaCola Darcel Franklin,** his cousin Nakia Kali said.

The 36-year-old truck driver was excited about his engagement to Franklin and their plans for a small, summer wedding.

Brewster's last Facebook exchange with Kali told the story, his cousin said. He wrote, "God is good. I love my life. This is mad cool."

"He loved NaCola. He *loved* NaCola," Kali said.

Franklin testified this week that she, too, was happy about their upcoming nuptials. That happiness ended abruptly early Aug. 11—the day they were to marry—when the former preschool teacher killed Brewster in the couple's Whitehall Township apartment as their children, Kali and his wife, Monique, looked on.

She stabbed Brewster in the chest and stomach with a kitchen knife, piercing his heart about six hours before the wedding. **Franklin, 32, was convicted Thursday of first-degree murder in his slaying following a three-day trial.** First-degree murder convictions carry a mandatory minimum sentence of life in prison without parole in Pennsylvania.

The Kalis were prosecution witnesses.

Brewster was a funny guy known for making wisecracks and easy to get along with, Kali said. "Anybody that met him would have liked him," he said.

Other men might have been daunted by the task of making a blended family work, but Brewster, a New York native, relished the prospect, Kali said. "He was serious about being family oriented."

He has a now one-year-old boy, BJ, with Franklin and a teenage son, William, from another relationship. William initially lived with his mother, but following her illness and death in 2011, moved in with his father, Kali said.

"His son, William, is the one that's hurting the most," he said. "William's mother passed away. Now, he had to witness his father die."

Franklin also has a son, Anthony, from another relationship. Brewster was making plans to adopt Anthony and had also welcomed his fiancée's young niece, India, into their home, his cousin said.

Kali said William is now in the care of his maternal grandmother, and the Franklin and Brewster's families have joint custody of BJ. Now that Franklin has been convicted, Brewster's relatives plan to seek full custody of the baby, he said.

Brewster worked 12 hours a day, six days a week, driving dedicated routes to Delaware, New Jersey, New York and Virginia for NFI, a national trucking and supply chain company, Franklin testified. He was on a work trip to California, her home state, when the couple met in 2009, she said. They settled down in Whitehall after NFI hired him in 2010.

Kali said Brewster enjoyed his job, despite the long hours, because it meant he could take good care of his family.

"He'd made it," Kali said.

Franklin's claim that Brewster beat her before she attacked him with the knife doesn't add up, Kali said. He and his wife were in a bedroom down the hall and would have heard the fight she described.

He also noted that police testified there were no signs of a scuffle in the master bedroom where Franklin said Brewster assaulted her. Kali said he begged her not to stab his cousin, but she was enraged and wouldn't listen to reason.

He and other relatives often speculate about what set her off.

"We believe Billy told her the wedding was off and she just couldn't take it," Kali said. "Whatever they were arguing about, she had it made up in her mind that she was going to kill him."

Although he's angry at Franklin and satisfied with the verdict, he feels sorry for her, too.

"I feel sorry for her because she had a glimpse of what her life was going to be," Kali said. "They went on cruises together. Billy was getting ready to adopt her son. He made enough money to support everyone in the household. They were saving up to buy a house. Everything was perfect."

www.ingramcontent.com/pod-product-compliance
Lightning Source LLC
Chambersburg PA
CBHW071413040426
42444CB00009B/2234